Blessings for
MY FRIEND

Artwork by **lori Siebert**

HARVEST HOUSE PUBLISHERS
EUGENE, OREGON

101 Inspirational Thoughts for My Friend

Text copyright © 2015 by Harvest House Publishers
Artwork copyright © by Olika Licensing, Inc./Lori Siebert

Published by Harvest House Publishers
Eugene, Oregon 97402
www.harvesthousepublishers.com

ISBN 978-0-7369-6453-1

Design and production by Garborg Design Works, Savage, Minnesota

Harvest House Publishers has made every effort to trace the ownership of all poems and quotes. In the event of a question arising from the use of a poem or quote, we regret any error made and will be pleased to make the necessary correction in future editions of this book.

All Scripture verses are taken from The Living Bible, Copyright © 1971. Used by permission of Tyndale House Publishers, Inc., Carol Stream, Illinois 60188. All rights reserved.

Printed in China

15 16 17 18 19 20 21 22 / LP / 10 9 8 7 6 5 4 3 2 1

Together

A true friend reaches for your hand and touches your heart.

AUTHOR UNKNOWN

1

live with
a light
heart

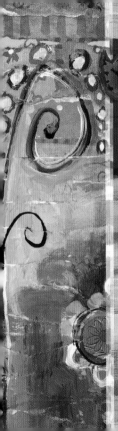

2

There are souls in this world who have the gift of finding joy everywhere, and leaving it behind them when they go.

FREDERICK WILLIAM FABER

3

Write it on your heart that every day is the best day in the year.

RALPH WALDO EMERSON

4

grow wise

5

Contentment is a pearl of great price, and whoever procures it at the expense of ten thousand desires makes a wise and happy purchase.

JOHN BALGUY

6

Life is made up, not of great sacrifices or duties, but of little things, in which smiles and kindnesses, and small obligations, given habitually, are what win and preserve the heart and secure comfort.

SIR HUMPHRY DAVY

7

He is a wise man who does not grieve for the things which he has not, but rejoices for those which he has.

EPICTETUS

8 notice beauty

9 In all ranks of life the human heart yearns for the beautiful; and the beautiful things that God makes are His gift to all alike.

HARRIET BEECHER STOWE

10 smile big & laugh lots

11

realize
your
strength

12

The soul is
strong that
trusts in
goodness.

PHILIP MASSINGER

13

*He fills me with strength and
protects me wherever I go.*

PSALM 18:32

15

Mistake not. Those pleasures are not pleasures that trouble the quiet and tranquility of thy life.

JEREMY TAYLOR

16

True silence is the rest of the mind; and is to the spirit what sleep is to the body, nourishment and refreshment.

WILLIAM PENN

17

pray often

18 Lord, make me according to thy heart.

BROTHER LAWRENCE

19 As well could you expect a plant to grow without air and water as to expect your heart to grow without prayer and faith.

CHARLES H. SPURGEON

20

dream big...
then make
it happen

21

In dreams
and in love
there are no
impossibilities.

JANOS ARANY

22

Every job is a
self-portrait of
the person who
did it. Autograph
your work with
excellence.

AUTHOR UNKNOWN

 23

To accomplish great things, we
must not only act, but also dream;
not only plan, but also believe.

ANATOLE FRANCE

take a walk

To find the universal elements enough; to find the air and the water exhilarating; to be refreshed by a morning walk or an evening saunter; to find a quest of wild berries more satisfying than a gift of tropic fruit; to be thrilled by the stars at night; to be elated over a bird's nest, or over a wildflower in spring— these are some of the rewards of the simple life.

JOHN BURROUGHS

26 *Everybody needs beauty as well as bread, places to play in and pray in, where nature may heal and give strength to body and soul alike.*

JOHN MUIR

27

learn
something
new

LO
VE

explore

experience

the journey.

28

Be someone's blessing.

29

The true source of cheerfulness is benevolence. The soul that perpetually overflows with kindness and sympathy will always be cheerful.

P. GODWIN

30

Do good, and leave behind you a monument of virtue that the storms of time can never destroy. Write your name in kindness, love, and mercy on the hearts of thousands you come in contact with year by year, and you will never be forgotten. Your name and your good deeds will shine as the stars of heaven.

THOMAS CARLYLE

31 express
yourself

32

There is no friend like an old friend who
has shared our morning days, no greeting
like his welcome, no homage like his praise.

OLIVER WENDELL HOLMES

33

But the mind never unbends itself so agreeably as in the conversation of a well-chosen friend. There is indeed no blessing of life that is any way comparable to the enjoyment of a discreet and virtuous friend. It eases and unloads the mind, clears and improves the understanding, engenders thoughts and knowledge, animates virtue and good resolutions, soothes and allays the passions, and finds employment for most of the vacant hours of life.

JOSEPH ADDISON

find the good

35

No matter what looms ahead, if you can eat today, enjoy the sunlight today, mix good cheer with friends today, enjoy it and bless God for it. Do not look back on happiness—or dream of it in the future. You are only sure of today; do not let yourself be cheated out of it.

HENRY WARD BEECHER

36 How goodness heightens beauty!

Hannah More

37 *Of all the best things on the earth,*
I hold that a faithful friend is the best.

Owen Meredith

38

Joy delights in joy.

WILLIAM SHAKESPEARE

39

don't take life
so seriously

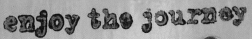

enjoy the journey

40

On with the dance!
Let joy be unconfined!

LORD BYRON

41

*That day is lost
on which one has
not laughed.*

FRENCH PROVERB

42 hug hello... and goodbye

43

Sweet is the hour that brings us home,
Where all will spring to meet us;
Where hands are striving as we come,
To be the first to greet us.

ELIZA COOK

44

Greet each other warmly.

THE BOOK OF 2 CORINTHIANS

45

I'm so glad that
you're my friend.
I know our
friendship will
never end.

ROBERT ALAN

46
drink lots of water

47

Live in each season as it passes; breathe the air, drink the drink, taste the fruit, and resign yourself to the influences of each.

HENRY DAVID THOREAU

48

forgive others— and yourself

49

Pray you now, forget and forgive.

WILLIAM
SHAKESPEARE

50 Trust the past to God's mercy, the present to God's love and the future to God's providence.

AUGUSTINE OF HIPPO

51 One word frees us of all the weight and pain of life: That word is love.

SOPHOCLES

52 enjoy the

53

Is it so small a thing
To have enjoyed the sun,
To have lived light in the spring,
To have loved, to have thought, to have done?

MATTHEW ARNOLD

moment

54 The art of being happy
lies in the power of
extracting happiness
from common things.

HENRY WARD BEECHER

55

discover joy

Treasure [fa·mi·ly]

56

We don't laugh because we're happy—we're happy because we laugh.

WILLIAM JAMES

57

It is not how much we have, but how much we enjoy, that makes happiness.

CHARLES H. SPURGEON

58

"Who are you, Pan?"
"I am youth, Eternal Youth!
I am the Sun rising, I am Poets singing,
I am the New World. I am a little bird
That has broken out of the egg,
I am Joy, Joy, Joy."

JAMES M. BARRIE, *PETER PAN*

take a deep

60

A thing of beauty is a joy forever;
Its loveliness increases;
It will never pass into nothingness;
But still will keep a bower quiet for us,
And a sleep full of sweet dreams,
And health, and quiet breathing.

JOHN KEATS

61

The fragrance always stays in the hand that gives the rose.

GEORGE WILLIAM CURTIS

62 LIVE GENEROUSLY

63

Guard well within yourself that treasure, kindness. Know how to give without hesitation, how to lose without regret, how to acquire without meanness.

GEORGE SAND

64 Sleep well

65

Then I lay down and slept in
peace and woke up safely, for
the Lord was watching over me.

THE BOOK OF PSALMS

66

let me help you

67

A reassuring presence,
A light when times are dark,
A hand reaching out,
Is what friendship is about.

AUTHOR UNKNOWN

68

*Hand grasps hand,
eye lights eye in
good friendship,
And great hearts expand
and grow one in the
sense of the world's life.*

ROBERT BROWNING

69

Hold a true
friend with both
your hands.

NIGERIAN PROVERB

70
Stand firm for what's right.

71

Whatever you do, you need courage. Whatever course you decide upon, there is always someone to tell you that you are wrong. There are always difficulties arising that tempt you to believe your critics are right. To map out a course of action and follow it to an end requires some of the same courage that a soldier needs. Peace has its victories, but it takes brave men and women to win them.

RALPH WALDO EMERSON

72 Sit and watch the sun set.

73 practice grace

74

Grace comes into the soul, as the morning sun into the world; first a dawning; then a light; and at last the sun in his full and excellent brightness.

THOMAS ADAMS

75

The only gift is a portion of thyself.

RALPH WALDO EMERSON

76

Try something different.

77

I never expect to see a perfect work from imperfect man.

ALEXANDER
HAMILTON

78

Well begun
is half done.

HORACE

79 A true friend is the greatest of all blessings, and that which we take the least care of all to acquire.

FRANCOIS DE LA ROÇHEFOUCAULD

80 count your blessings

81 Faith is the root of all blessings.

JEREMY TAYLOR

82

read a book

83

The love of learning,
The sequestered nooks,
And all the sweet serenity of books.

HENRY WADSWORTH LONGFELLOW

84

Are we not like two
volumes of one book?

Marceline Desbordes-Valmore

85 Let God help.

86

He sendeth sun, he sendeth shower,
Alike they're needful for the flower;
And joys and tears alike are sent
To give the soul fit nourishment.

SARAH FLOWER ADAMS

87

There is a comfort in the strength of love;
'Twill make a thing endurable, which else
Would overset the brain, or break the heart

WILLIAM WORDSWORTH

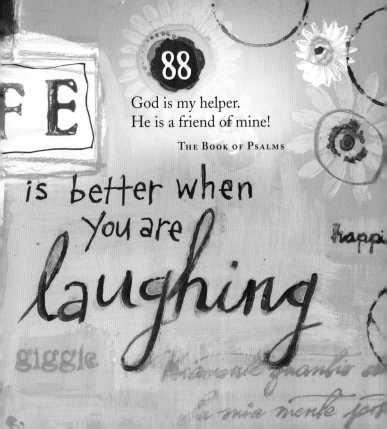

FE

88

God is my helper.
He is a friend of mine!

THE BOOK OF PSALMS

is better when
you are

laughing

giggle   happi

exchange fear
89 for peace

The foolish fears of what might happen,
I cast them all away
Among the clover-scented grass,
Among the new-mown hay,
Among the husking of the corn,
Where drowsy poppies nod
Where ill thoughts die and good are born—
Out in the fields with God.

ELIZABETH BARRETT BROWNING
AND LOUISE IMOGEN GUINEY

91 When I am afraid,
I will put my confidence in you.
Yes, I will trust the promises of God.

THE BOOK OF PSALMS

Aspire

inspire

92

play
more

93

Be merry if
you are wise.

Marcus Valerius
Martialis

SHARE *goodness*

94 Man could direct his ways by plain reason, and support his life by tasteless food, but God has given us wit, and flavor, and brightness, and laughter to enliven the days of man's pilgrimage.

SYDNEY SMITH

96

Nurture your
minds with
great thoughts;
to believe in the
heroic makes
heroes.

BENJAMIN DISRAELI

97

Charity is
a virtue of
the heart.

JOSEPH ADDISON

98

remember
that I
love you—
always

99

*Yesterday brought the
beginning, tomorrow
brings the end, but
somewhere in the
middle we've become
the best of friends.*

AUTHOR UNKNOWN

100

A true friend…advises justly, assists
readily, adventures boldly, takes all
patiently, defends courageously, and
continues a friend unchangeably.

WILLIAM PENN

101

Oh, be my friend,
and teach me
to be thine!

RALPH WALDO EMERSON